WESSEX GARDENS PRIMARY SCHOOL
Wessex Gardens
Golders Green
LONDON NW11 9RR
Tel: 020 8455 9572

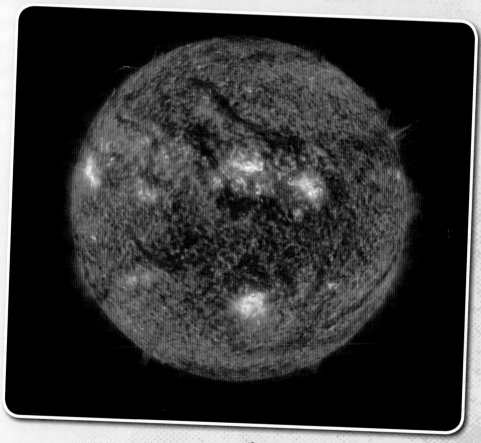

Fact Cat

THE SUN

Alice Harman

WAYLAND

FACT CAT

Get your paws on this fantastic new mega-series from Wayland!

Join our Fact Cat on a journey of fun learning about every subject under the sun!

First published in 2014 by Wayland
© Wayland 2014

Wayland
Hachette Children's Books
338 Euston Road
London NW1 3BH

Wayland Australia
Level 17/207 Kent Street
Sydney NSW 2000

Produced for Wayland by
White-Thomson Publishing Ltd
www.wtpub.co.uk
+44 (0) 843 208 7460

Editor: Alice Harman
Design: Rocket Design (East Anglia) Ltd
Fact Cat illustrations: Shutterstock/Julien Troneur
Other illustrations: Stefan Chabluk/Bill Donohue
Consultant: Kate Ruttle

A catalogue for this title is available from the British Library

ISBN: 978 0 7502 8223 9
eBook ISBN: 978 0 7502 8533 9

Dewey Number: 523.7-dc23

10 9 8 7 6 5 4 3 2

Wayland is a division of Hachette Children's Books,
an Hachette UK company.
www.hachette.co.uk

Printed and bound in China

Picture and illustration credits:
Chabluk, Stefan: 10, 14; Donohoe, William: 4-5;
Dreamstime: Alessandro Bagalini 5, Rachel Travis 8,
Uko_jesita 9, Rinus Baak 11, John Wollwerth 12,
Ioana Grecu 13, Burkhard Behling 15, Constantin Opris 20;
ESA/NASA/SOHO: cover and title page;
Getty Images: Akiko Aoki 17; Shutterstock: Triff 4;
Wikimedia: Luc Viatour/www.lucnix.be 16, Polarlicht_2 18,
NASA Goddard Space Flight Center 19, Mysid 21.

Every effort has been made to clear copyright.
Should there be any inadvertent omission,
please apply to the publisher for rectification.

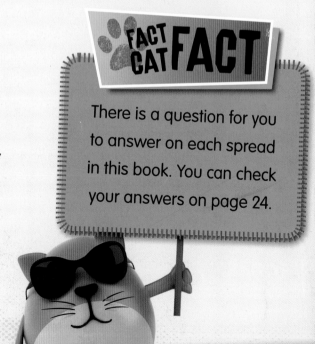

FACT CAT FACT

There is a question for you to answer on each spread in this book. You can check your answers on page 24.

CONTENTS

WHAT IS THE SUN?

The Sun is a star. Stars are huge balls of very hot **gas**. The Sun is the closest star to Earth, which is our **planet**. The Earth moves around, or **orbits**, the Sun.

The Sun gives out heat and light. Plants and animals need these things to stay alive. Without the Sun, nothing on Earth could survive.

The **glow** of light from the Sun looks different to the light from other stars. This is because the Sun is much closer to Earth than they are. Find out how far away from Earth the Sun is.

The Sun looks different to other stars in the sky because it is so much closer to Earth than they are. This also makes the Sun look much bigger than other stars, but it is actually a medium-sized star.

THE SUN IN SPACE

Eight planets orbit the Sun, including Earth. The closer a planet is to the Sun, the hotter it is there. Earth is the only planet that is neither too hot nor too cold for living things to survive there.

A solar system is the name for a star and the planets and other objects that orbit it. Try to draw your own picture of our solar system.

Saturn

Uranus

Neptune

FACT CAT FACT

A **million** Earths could fit inside the Sun. However, 10 **billion** Suns could fit inside the biggest known star in the **universe**. This star is called VY Canis Majoris.

Mercury

Sun

Earth

Venus

Mars

Earth's moon

Jupiter

The Sun doesn't stay still in one place. It moves very slowly around the centre of our galaxy. A galaxy is a group of billions of stars and other objects.

Our solar system is in a galaxy called the Milky Way. We can see other parts of the Milky Way from Earth. It looks like a light, dusty-looking stripe in the night sky.

SUNLIGHT

Plants use sunlight to make their own food. This is called photosynthesis. Animals cannot make their own food in this way, but they do eat plants. This means that animals also need the Sun for their food.

Aphids eat plants, and ladybirds eat aphids. If there was no Sun, there would be no plants. This would mean no aphids, and no ladybirds.

ladybird

aphid

We can use energy from sunlight to run machines such as televisions. Special dark-coloured **panels** catch sunlight and turn it into **electricity**. This electricity moves through **wires** and into the machines.

solar panels

Solar power is what we call the energy from sunlight. Try to find out why using solar power is better for Earth than burning **coal** and **oil**.

FACT CAT FACT

Sunlight keeps us alive, but it can also be very dangerous. You must never look at the Sun, as it could badly hurt your eyes. Strong sunlight can also burn your skin, so you need to wear **sun lotion**.

DAY AND NIGHT

Earth spins around as it orbits the Sun. It takes 24 hours for Earth to spin round once. The Sun shines on the part of Earth that faces it. It is daytime in the countries in this part of Earth.

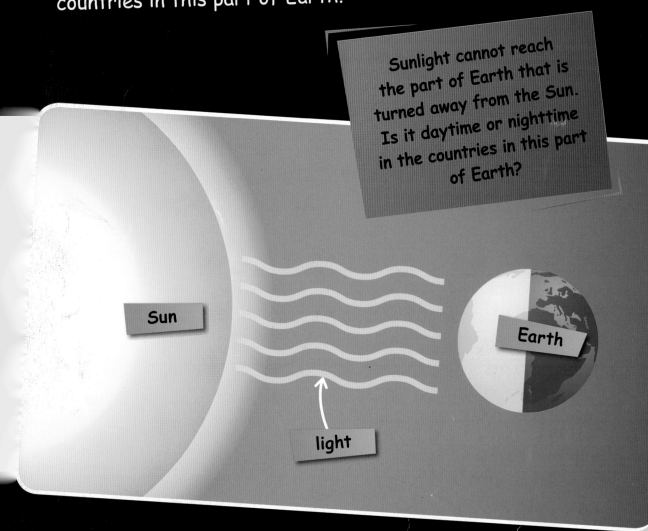

Sunlight cannot reach the part of Earth that is turned away from the Sun. Is it daytime or nighttime in the countries in this part of Earth?

Sun

Earth

light

The Sun gives out heat as well as light. This means that it is hotter in the day than it is at night. In areas of Earth that get very hot, animals sometimes move around at night because it is cooler.

Burrowing owls live in hot areas such as **deserts**. They mostly stay underground where it is cooler during the hottest part of the day.

FACT CAT FACT

It can be extremely hot in the desert during the day, but then much colder at night. The Mojave Desert is one of the hottest places on Earth, but at night it can be freezing cold there.

SUNRISE AND SUNSET

In the morning, the Sun seems to rise in the sky. But it is Earth that moves, not the Sun. We see more of the Sun as our part of Earth turns towards it.

As our part of Earth turns towards the Sun, more light and heat from the Sun reaches us. It is brighter and warmer after sunrise than before it.

At the end of the day, the Sun seems to drop lower and lower in the sky until it disappears. This is because our part of Earth is turning away from the Sun.

As our part of the Earth turns away from the Sun, it becomes dark there. When this happens, is it hotter or cooler in this area? Why?

FACT CAT FACT

Light has to travel further from the Sun to reach Earth at sunrise and sunset, because the Earth is partly turned away from the Sun. This makes the light appear in bright colours such as red, orange, yellow and pink.

SEASONS

Earth takes one year to travel all the way around the Sun. Earth is **tilted** as it moves. This means that each side of Earth is tilted towards the Sun for half a year, and tilted away from the Sun for half a year.

When a side of Earth is tilted towards the Sun, it is closer to it. This means it gets more sunlight and heat. It is summer on that side.

Earth

north

south

light

Sun

FACT CAT FACT

When it is summer for one side of the Earth, there are more hours of sunlight each day. As this side of Earth is tilted towards the Sun, it faces the Sun for longer as it spins round.

There are four seasons. They are spring, summer, autumn and winter. In winter, there is less light and heat from the Sun. Plants need sunlight to make food, so many of them die or stop growing in winter.

In winter, many trees lose their leaves. These are called deciduous trees. Some trees keep their leaves in winter. Find out what these trees are called.

SOLAR ECLIPSES

At least twice a year, the Moon passes between Earth and the Sun. The Moon blocks the Sun's light, and it becomes dark on Earth. This is called a solar eclipse.

The Moon is much, much smaller than the Sun. It can block out the Sun's light because it is a lot closer to Earth than the Sun and so it appears bigger.

This boy is safely watching a solar eclipse by using special eclipse glasses. Find out when the next solar eclipse is in your country.

You must never look straight at the Sun during a solar eclipse. The Sun's light is extremely bright and can very badly hurt your eyes. You need to use special equipment to watch solar eclipses.

FACT CAT FACT

The Moon is very, very slowly moving away from Earth. In around 600 million years, it will be too small to completely block the Sun's light. This means there will be no more solar eclipses.

AURORAS AND SOLAR FLARES

Auroras are streams of coloured light that move across the night sky. They appear when **rays** from the Sun hit Earth's atmosphere. The atmosphere is a thin layer of gases that **surrounds** Earth.

Auroras can only be seen in certain countries. When they appear in countries in the North, they are called the Northern Lights. Find three countries where the Northern Lights appear.

The Sun always burns brightly, but sometimes there are sudden flashes of extra brightness on the Sun. These are called solar flares. They are **explosions** that push out burning gas into space.

When solar flares happen on a part of the Sun that faces Earth, a lot of energy travels towards our planet. Earth's atmosphere stops most of this energy from reaching us.

FACT CAT FACT

Solar flares can make auroras appear in places where they are not normally seen. There were a lot of solar flares in October 2013. People saw auroras in Ireland and the middle of the USA.

TOO HOT FOR EARTH?

Earth needs heat and light from the Sun, but not too much. Earth's atmosphere helps to **control** how much heat and light we get. **Pollution** is damaging the atmosphere, so it doesn't work as well.

Try to find out how factories, cars and people cause pollution. Then find three ways in which we can help the planet by **reducing** pollution.

Sun

This picture shows the Sun next to a red giant star. Billions of years in the future, the Sun will become a red giant too.

red giant star

The Sun has very slowly been getting bigger and brighter since it was first formed. When the Sun becomes a red giant, we will have to live on another planet!

FACT CAT FACT

Stars can explode with a huge burst of bright light. This is called a supernova. The Sun will never explode like this, as it isn't heavy enough. However, there is one supernova every second in our galaxy.

QUIZ

Try to answer the questions below. Look back through the book to help you. Check your answers on page 24.

1 Can animals and plants survive without the Sun's heat and light?

a) animals can survive, but plants cannot

b) plants can survive, but animals cannot

c) no, neither animals nor plants can survive

2 How long does Earth take to travel all the way around the Sun?

a) one day

b) one month

c) one year

3 The Sun is the biggest star in the universe? True or not true?

a) true

b) not true

4 Is Earth the closest planet to the Sun?

a) yes

b) no

5 What is the name of our galaxy?

a) The Cheesy Path

b) The Buttery Road

c) The Milky Way

GLOSSARY

billion a thousand million (1,000,000,000)

control to make something do what you want

desert hot, dry area

electricity type of power or energy that is used to work machines like televisions and to give light and heat

explosion when something blows up with a loud bang

gas form of material that doesn't have a fixed shape or size, like air

glow a shining light, often given out by something very hot

million a thousand thousands (1,000,000)

orbit when an object in space moves in a curved path around another object

panel flat board

planet large object in space that moves around a star

pollution dirty, harmful substance such as smoke or car fumes

ray beam, or straight line, of light or heat

reduce make something less

solid form of material that you can normally see and touch, like rock

star large object in space that is made of burning gas

sun lotion cream or spray that you put on your skin to protect it from the harmful rays of the Sun

surface the top layer of an object

surround form a circle all around something

tilted when something is a bit tipped over on its side

universe everything in space, including the Earth, the Sun, and all the stars and planets

wires long, thin strips of metal through which electricity passes

INDEX

ANSWERS

Pages 5–20

page 5: The Sun is 149,600,000 km (92,957,130 miles) away from Earth. That's further than travelling around the world 3700 times!

page 9: Three reasons are: 1) coal and oil make the air dirty and bad to breathe, but solar power doesn't; 2) coal and oil damage the atmosphere, but solar power doesn't; 3) coal and oil supplies will run out soon, but the Sun won't!

page 10: It is nighttime.

page 13: It is cooler. In the day, heat from the Sun can reach us.

page 15: They are evergreen trees.

page 18: They appear in the northern areas of Sweden, Norway, Finland, Greenland, Canada, Iceland, Russia, Alaska (part of the USA) and Scotland.

page 20: Three possible suggestions are: 1) walk, cycle or take public transport instead of going by car; 2) recycle rubbish instead of throwing it away; 3) turn off lights when you leave a room.

Quiz answers

1   c) No, neither animals nor plants can survive.

2   c) one year

3   b) not true

4   b) No, it is the third closest planet.

5   c) The Milky Way.

OTHER TITLES IN THE FACT CAT SERIES...

UNITED KINGDOM

FACT CAT
ENGLAND

9780750284332

9780750284394

FACT CAT
SCOTLAND
Alice Harman

FACT CAT
NORTHERN IRELAND

Alice Harman

9780750284400

9780750284387

FACT CAT
WALES

Alice Harman

COUNTRIES

FACT CAT
FRANCE

Alice Harman

9780750282123

9780750282130

FACT CAT
BRAZIL

Alice Harman

FACT CAT
GHANA

Alice Harman

9780750282154

9780750282147

FACT CAT
ITALY
Alice Harman

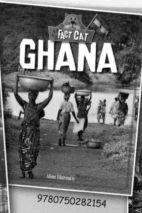

WAYLAND